SCOUT&JET

INTO THE GOBI DESERT

To Layla,
Always foster your curiosity
Theophany Eystathioy

Theophany Eystathioy

Illustrated by:
Lisa Thompson

Edited by:
Cheri Hanson

A Little PhDs Book
www.littlephds.com

A Little PhDs Book
www.littlephds.com

SCOUT & JET
SERIES

THE ADVENTURE BEGINS
INTO THE GOBI DESERT

Library & Archives Canada Cataloging – in –Publication Data
Eystathioy, Theophany

Scout and Jet: Into the Gobi Desert/ written by Theophany Eystathioy; illustrated by Lisa Thompson

Summary: Follow the adventures of Scout and Jet, who travel back in time to meet real historical figures whose discoveries advanced our scientific knowledge. In this book, the kids meet Roy Chapman Andrews – an explorer and scientist who may have inspired the Indiana Jones films. – Provided by publisher

ISBN 978-0-9952552-3-4 (ebook)
ISBN 978-0-9952552-2-7 (pbk)

To my husband and sister,
your support has meant the world to me.
-T.E

CHAPTER 1

"**C**an you hear it?" Scout asked her brother. Jet nodded, listening carefully. "It's that way," he motioned to the right. As they hurried along, Jet tripped on a tree root sticking out of the ground.

"I think we're getting closer," Scout said, glancing back at Jet as he stumbled. She could feel the warm sun on her face. It was a clear day without any clouds in the sky. Massive trees surrounded them. They were deep inside the forest. Well, no. Not really, Scout could still see the cottage.

They were already a few days into their vacation – and what felt like a lifetime without electronics. No Wi-Fi, TV or computers, either. Just board games. After rolling dice and moving game pieces for hours, they needed something else to do. Charm, the older lady who owned the cottage, had suggested they take a walk through the small forest behind the house. It was that or more board games. The kids chose the walk.

The cottage looked a bit smaller now. They were climbing uphill in search of what sounded like a flushing toilet. They desperately wanted to find where it was coming from. "We must be getting closer. It's getting louder now." Scout increased her pace and Jet followed close behind. Then they saw it – a stream running with cold mountain water!

Finally, Scout thought as she took off her shoes and socks. She felt a gush of water hit her face. "Hey, don't splash!" she said to her brother.

Jet was already walking in the cold stream. "This is awesome. My feet are finally cooling off." Suddenly Jet went quiet. "You don't think there are any strange creatures lurking in here, do you?" He was examining the water carefully. "Like flesh-eating fish or something?"

"Oh, you never know." Scout replied with a serious face. Jet jumped out of the water like a flash.

Scout grinned.

"Not funny, Scout!" Jet put on his socks and shoes and stretched out beside the stream. "I'm pooped. Hiking is hard work. We've been gone like, what, half an hour?"

Scout was quiet.

"Hello? Earth to Scout. Do you hear me?" Jet emphasized each word, trying to get her attention. But Scout was staring off into the distance.

"What are you looking at?" Jet followed his sister's gaze.

"What is that?" Scout pointed to a hill beyond the stream. "Is that a cave?"

Off to her right, Scout could see a visible opening in the hill. Vines encircled the gap and a few trees dotted either side of the entranceway.

"Are those steps?" Jet asked incredulously.

"Yeah, and I think it leads to that cave." Scout pointed at the hill.

"Maybe we should just leave?" Scout was secretly hoping Jet would agree.

"Definitely not!" Jet jumped a few steps ahead of her. "Charm said that the forest here is fun and safe. Remember?"

"Come on. It's not like we haven't had adventures before." Jet was excited. His mind was already racing. Who knew what could be inside the cave? He was hoping for bats, but there was no way he would share that thought with Scout.

"All right, fine." Scout followed her brother. When they reached the steps, Scout peered into the dark

mouth of the cave. "I don't think we should go in. It's soooo dark."

Jet shrugged and continued on, slowly.

With her eyes fixed on the cave, Scout tripped and stepped on something. She knelt down and examined the ground. "What a coincidence," she murmured to herself. "Jet, look – a flashlight."

Jet turned around. "Wow! That's so weird," he said, snatching the flashlight away from her.

"I don't think so," Scout declared. "I found it, so I get to use it." She grabbed the flashlight back from Jet and switched it on as they entered the cave. Thankfully, it worked. Scout scanned the inside of the cave, from the floor to the ceiling, and left to right on the walls. There was enough space for them both to fit comfortably. And there was plenty of headroom.

"How far do you think this goes?" Scout asked, shining her light into the distance. Only blackness beckoned. Scout listened carefully for any strange noises, but all she could hear was her own breathing.

"Who knows? Maybe we'll find treasure." *Or bats, or even snakes,* Jet thought silently to himself.

As Scout and Jet shuffled forward, the darkness seemed to subside a little. Cracks in the cave walls and ceiling were letting in more light. Scout began to relax until she recalled that bears hibernate in caves. It wasn't winter, but this could still be a bear's bedroom. She reached for Jet's arm to yank him back, then froze. So did Jet. The cracks in the right wall were getting larger. Wider beams of light shone through, converging on a single point.

"Is that what I think it is?" Scout asked in disbelief.

"Woohoo! It's treasure!" Jet ran over to a large black box perched on a wooden table. Jet touched the box and tried to open it.

"Wait!" Scout commanded. "Don't!"

"What? Why not?" Jet stopped for a moment, then continued to investigate the box.

"What if it's booby trapped?" Scout asked, remembering an Indiana Jones movie they had watched with their parents.

"As if!" Jet snorted, then paused and looked around the cave for a moment. "I am going to open it. Just keep watch."

The lid was heavier than Jet expected. As the box opened, a gush a wind blew through the cave. Both kids jumped in surprise. But Scout jumped further. Creepy crawlers were emerging from the box. Spiders first, then beetles.

"Gross!" Scout exclaimed. Jet took a step back. A moment, then two went by.

After it seemed like the last bug had scurried off, Jet approached the box and carefully looked inside.

"Scout. Look at this." Jet beckoned his sister forward. Scout stepped around the beetles crawling on the ground.

"Come on. Look at this," Jet motioned.

Scout peered at the box, and then slowly glanced inside. "Is that… is that a book?"

"Yeah," said Jet. Although I was hoping for treasure." He wiped the top of the book with his hands. A puff of dust rose into the air.

AH-CHOO! Jet wiped his nose with his arm. *Why did they keep finding books that were so old and dusty?* he thought, annoyed.

Scout carefully inspected the box; she needed to make sure that no bugs were left behind. Deciding it was safe, she lifted the book out of the box. It was big and surprisingly heavy. The cover was all black.

There was no title and no author listed. *Strange!* Scout thought. Everything about this was strange. In fact, everything about this vacation at the cottage was weird.

"We're taking the book?" Jet asked.

"We'll return it," said Scout. "I just want to see what it's about."

Jet moved to sit on the floor of the cave.

"Not here," instructed Scout "There are still bugs crawling around. Let's take it outside."

The kids left the cave and descended the stairs, settling under a shady tree. Scout gently laid the book on the ground and sat down. Her brother remained on his feet.

"Jet? What are you doing?"

"I feel better if I'm standing."

"Really? It's not as if we could wind up on a cliff or something!"

She has a point, Jet thought to himself, then sat down. He grabbed her arm.

"Ow! What's that for?"

"I just don't know what's going to happen!"

Scout rolled her eyes, but she couldn't blame her brother. She was nervous and excited at the same time. If their past adventure had taught them anything, books were not simply books in this place.

Here goes nothing! Scout opened the book and began reading the page in front of her.

*Welcome back, Scout and Jet. Are you ready
for an adventure? Want to go back in time?*

Scout took a deep breath and gulped. Jet clutched his sister's arm.

"How does the book know our names?" Jet whispered. He looked at his sister.

"I don't know," she whispered back. She turned her attention back to the page.

*Come and meet Roy Chapman Andrews...
and hold on tight.*

The book is giving us a warning! Scout thought. But before she could say a word, a strong wind blew though the forest. The tree branches bent over, leaves fell to the ground, and the sky started to darken.

Then whoosh .....

CHAPTER 2

"**W**...o...w Nelly... W...h...e...r...e... are... w...e?" Jet's voice wavered as he closed his eyes in the bright sun. He just couldn't look.

Scout saw the horizon moving up and down, up and down. Then she saw a brown hump moving up and down, up and down. She was on top of something. Her mind raced. It wasn't a horse, and it wasn't a donkey. What was she bouncing on? Then she figured it out.

They were on camels! *Holy tzatziki sauce,* they were riding camels. She had seen a camel before at the zoo. But this clearly wasn't the zoo. Scout couldn't figure out where they were – and she didn't care! She just preferred adventures where her feet were touching the ground. She wanted off this creature! Suddenly, her camel started to slow down, almost as if it could hear her thoughts. Scout noticed that Jet's camel was also slowing down. She realized that there were many, many, many other camels nearby. *Holy guacamole. Where are we?* Her camel made a funny noise and then spat.

"Oh donkey, we're on camels!" Jet said as his animal pulled up next to Scout. He looked paler than usual.

Riding a camel was not the same as riding a pony or a go-cart.

AH-CHOO!

Jet sneezed again. "I think I'm allergic to camels, too," he said, wiping his nose with his arm. He sneezed again. This time it was so fierce that he almost lost his balance.

Scout glanced away from her brother and realized that she was sweating. Scout looked up into the blazing sun. There wasn't one cloud in the sky. *Where are we?* She squinted her eyes and surveyed the landscape. There were camels and sand everywhere. No trees in sight. Scout was sure that this was the desert. Scout turned to Jet and saw that he was sliding left and right, trying to get off his camel. Scout smirked.

"Since when do we allow children on an expedition?" someone bellowed.

"Stowaways!" another voice shouted.

"Stowaways?" Jet whispered to Scout. *We aren't stowaways,* Jet thought to himself. They had just been walking in the woods.

"Okay, kids. Down you go," said a tall man wearing a black hat. Scout looked down as her camel began sinking toward the sand.

"Whoa!" she yelled. The camel's sudden kneeling caught Scout by surprise. Jet's camel also knelt to the ground.

The next thing Jet knew, his feet were touching the ground. His legs buckled for a microsecond. The tall man stared at him and his sister.

Scout thought about how much her butt hurt. But that thought was short lived. *What's that smell?* she wondered, looking around. Then she saw the source. It was camel poop – and lots of it!

"P.U!" Jet blurted out. "Camel poop. Yuck!"

The man ignored Jet.

"Now, how did you two get here? We just entered the Gobi Desert. This is no place for children!" He frowned as he spoke.

Someone else asked how the kids had gone undetected.

"Umm…. We…" Scout thought she should say something.

How were they going to explain this? Scout looked at Jet, but he was no help. Her brother was staring at the sky with a smirk on his face; he obviously found the whole thing amusing.

Jet *was* amused. There were several cars parked next to a whole bunch of camels – and they were in the middle of nowhere. "One of these things is not like the other," he hummed under his breath.

"So… are you looking for an adventure?" asked the man with the hat. This time he was smiling. Then he lowered his voice. "Don't worry, kids. You remind me of…. well, of me when I was your age. If I had seen camels and a caravan I would have joined them, too," he said, grinning.

"We can't keep going with these kids, Roy," said a gruff-looking man wearing a bandana.

The man in the hat rubbed his jaw.

"You're right," he said. "Okay, men. Keep on going. I will catch up with you. I am going to take these kids back to town. I'm sure their parents are frantic. We will find them." He smiled as he turned toward Scout and Jet.

Roy motioned for them to follow him.

"Do we need to ride the camels again?" Jet asked, secretly hoping that he would never, ever have to ride another camel.

The man laughed. "Why ride camels when you have this motor car? It will get us there faster." He opened the door and gestured for the kids to get in. "People thought I was crazy to bring motor cars on this expedition, but I think I made the right choice."

Jet looked at Scout and Scout shrugged. What choice did they have? She definitely did not want to go further into the desert. It was so hot and she was so thirsty. It would be better to ride in a car with air conditioning.

"Sorry," the man said, glancing at the kids in the back. "I didn't introduce myself. My name is Roy Chapman Andrews. You can call me Roy."

Scout paused. She recognized his name from the book. She elbowed Jet. "I'm Scout and this is my brother Jet." Scout wiped her forehead. Her throat felt parched.

"Nice to meet you kids. Here, have some water." Roy handed them a weird leather container. It looked strange, but the water was nice and cool. After her thirst was quenched, Scout passed the container to Jet.

Jet noticed that the car looked really different than the one his parents drove. For one thing, there was no visible roof. Jet's mom had taught him all about cars. He guessed that this was probably an old Dodge. He would bet Scout's rock collection on it. "I don't think this car has air conditioning," Jet whispered to his sister.

Scout just sighed. She was so hot. Even her feet were sweating.

"Don't worry, kids," said Roy, misinterpreting Scout's sigh. "I will get you back to your parents. You will be home in no time." Roy tipped the front end of his ranger hat.

"What year is this?" Jet had to ask. He was pretty sure that they had travelled back in time. The car was so unusual. On their last adventure, they went all the way back to 1811.

"Son, did you hit your head when you climbed down from that camel?" Roy peered back at Jet. "The year is 1923, kid."

"You said we're in the Gobi Desert?" Scout asked.

"That's right. The Gobi Desert of Mongolia."

Roy started the vehicle. He noticed the kids looking at him intently. "I am leading a big expedition." The car bumped along over the sand, which surprised Jet. How come it didn't get stuck? There were no roads in sight.

"I am leading a scientific expedition," Roy clarified.

"Ex – pe – di - tion?" Jet asked, struggling to pronounce the word.

"It's the largest expedition to ever leave the United States," said Roy. "Well, it is a bit crazy. We have about 40 men, eight cars, and over a hundred camels."

"Wow," said Jet, trying to do the math in his head.

"We are looking for very old things, like fossils and bones." Roy paused. "Do you kids know what fossils are?"

Jet nodded, and thought back to their last adventure with Mary Anning.

"The Gobi Desert is a dinosaur graveyard," said Roy. Jet shuddered at the word *graveyard*. "But this is no place for kids. The desert seems to have a mind of its own. It is a dangerous place. There are crazy sandstorms, and the winds mixed with sand are so powerful that it is hard to breathe or see. There are also hot days and freezing cold nights," Roy paused for a moment and looked back at the kids.

"The other night, we had vipers in our campsite. Really big snakes!" He mimed a long reptile with his hands. "Good thing it was cold that night, because it slowed them down. I hate to think what would have happened during the day. Anyhow, I think we killed over 40 of them."

Scout looked pale and swallowed hard. Jet just smiled. He thought vipers were cool.

Roy laughed at their different reactions. "Jet, I have to say that I am with your sister on that one. I really despise snakes." He winked at Scout.

It was getting harder to have a conversation. The road (or lack of it) was so bumpy. Jet was starting to feel a bit nauseated. The car was travelling over a rough patch, hitting boulders and rocks. It seemed like forever, but to Jet's relief, they finally made it to even ground.

Suddenly, Scout jerked her head around. Out of nowhere, animals – and lots of them – were jumping next to the car. "Gazelles," Roy said, preempting their question. "You never see these in the city. They are magnificent animals that roam the desert without a care in the world." Jet and Scout stood up to get a better look. There were dozens of gazelles in front, beside and behind the car. Scout took it all in. As quickly as the gazelles came into view, they seemed to get sucked into the faraway horizon.

"The desert is pretty amazing," said Roy. "As a child, I dreamed of traveling to strange places. I only wanted to be outdoors and exploring. I read lots of books about natural history when I was your age." Scout and Jet listened intently as Roy continued. "I wanted to travel the world. How I ached to do this when I was a kid." Roy took a swig of water and returned the bottle to the seat beside him. "Now I am traveling the world in search of animals and their remains."

Jet and Scout looked at each other. They understood what he was saying. He was searching for fossils, just like Mary Anning was on their last adventure. Scout looked around. The desert really was beautiful and so different from anything she had ever seen before. There were rolling hills of sand and rock. In the distance, she could see reddish cliffs. The desert was vast. Roy began to steer the car up a hill. The climb up was unnerving. All she could see was clear blue sky. Halfway down the hill, the car jerked.

Jet noticed that Roy had come to a complete stop. *Maybe gazelles were blocking his path,* Jet thought to himself.

Roy was looking at something. Jet stood up and followed his gaze. Up ahead were about four men, dressed in weird clothing and sitting on horses.

"Who are they?" Scout asked.

CHAPTER 3

"**B**andits," Roy said, calmly.

"Bandits!" Jet gulped. *This did not sound good.*

"Yes, these armed men are up to no good. They obviously want to block our path."

Roy looked back at the kids. "I have a plan. Listen carefully and do everything I say." He pressed on the gas pedal and the car quickly gained speed. "Get down!"

"Huh?" said Jet.

Before Jet could ask what he meant, Scout pushed his head down. The car was moving fast. They both looked up and for a split second, they saw Roy driving straight toward the bandits. Scout realized the bandits had rifles. Jet must have noticed, too, because both kids caught their breath and grabbed the back seat to steady themselves. When Scout looked up again, after what seemed like forever, the bandits had dispersed – all except one. Roy slowed down but didn't stop. He pulled out his revolver and fired a few shots at one of the bandits riding close to the car. Roy aimed at his hat. The bandit took off quickly.

"That should do it. I really didn't like his hat," Roy said, laughing and adjusted his own after putting his revolver away. "They won't bother us again."

This was turning out to be a crazy adventure.

"Like I said, this place is dangerous. If vipers don't get you, the bandits will try." He looked back at Scout and Jet. "You kids did good."

They drove for what seemed like forever.

"I am going to stop the car," said Roy. "There is something I want to show you." He pointed to a small hill just a few meters away. "We found something the other day and I think you kids will find it pretty interesting."

"Really?" Scout and Jet said in unison. They were intrigued.

Roy stopped the car at the bottom of the hill. Scout touched the sand with her hands. It was burning hot. There was no breeze, and sweat was pooling on her forehead. Their shoes dug deep in the sand as they walked up the hill.

When they finally got to the top, the kids were slightly ahead of Roy. They scanned their surroundings. The desert was huge.

"Watch your step." Roy had caught up to them now and put his hand out to block the kids from advancing.

"Look at this!" Roy crouched down. Scout joined him. Jet moved in to take a closer look, but after seeing

Scout flinch from the hot sand, he was careful not to sit down.

"So what do you kids think this is?" Roy asked. There was a circular structure in the middle of the sand, with more circular objects inside. After a few moments, Jet was the first to speak.

"That looks like eggs," Jet said, squinting for a better look.

"Really large eggs," Scout agreed.

"Well done," Roy said, pointing to the circular objects. "This is a nest of dinosaur eggs." The kids looked at one another. They knew dinosaurs came from eggs, because they had learned about it at school. And now they were looking right at a nest! Roy adjusted his ranger hat.

"This suggests that dinosaurs were not born alive, but hatched from eggs. Scientists have been asking this question, and now we have the answer."

Scout shifted her gaze. She noticed a strange pattern in the sand, close to the eggs. As she examined it more carefully, Scout could see what looked like a skull. *It's a fossil,* she thought to herself. *Ah-ha! Thank you, Mary Anning!* Scout was proud of her deduction and thought back to their first adventure. Roy came over and stood next to Scout.

"Very observant, Scout." He ran his hand over the fossil, using his finger to point out smaller details. "This is a dinosaur skull, and this here is its skeleton. It looks like a new dinosaur species. It is strange to find a fossil so close to the eggs. Perhaps it was trying to take one for dinner."

Jet and Scout stared at what they had found. Dinosaur eggs, and now a dinosaur fossil. How cool!

"Is there a baby dinosaur inside?" Jet asked.

Roy removed his hat to wipe his forehead. "You mean an embryo. That's the word we use to describe the animal inside an un-hatched egg."

Roy opened up a couple of the eggs that were already cracked.

"It's a great question. But nope! No embryo. That would be amazing, wouldn't it?" Roy gently placed the eggs back where he found them.

"If there was an embryo inside, we could figure out what dinosaur they came from," said Roy. He stood up and they walked back to the car. "We need to understand what was here before us." Roy motioned to the desert all around them. "We can only figure this out by studying fossils. Fossils are the ghost whisperers of the past." Roy stopped and stared at into the horizon.

"We just need to find them." His expression became somber for a moment. And just as quickly, a grin spread over his face.

"Okay, lesson over." He winked at the kids. "Time to get you back home."

CHAPTER 4

Jet felt a strong wind rise up out of nowhere, and he scrambled to stand next to Scout. The next thing they knew, the kids were sitting on the forest floor.

"Wow!" Jet said.

"We're back," Scout added, scanning her surroundings.

Jet suddenly remembered what happened last time. Scout was already moving away from the book.

Jet was happy to do the same. They looked at each other. The page in front of them was blank.

"It's your turn to ask a question. I did it last time," Scout reminded her brother.

"Fine. Okay, here goes. Was that really a nest of dinosaur eggs?" The kids took a deep breath and waited. Words began to appear, one by one, on the blank page.

Yes. They recovered over 20 eggs. It was a very important discovery.

"Was that a dinosaur fossil next to the eggs?" Scout asked.

Yes. That fossil belonged to a dinosaur, which was later named Oviraptor; it means egg thief. They initially thought this dinosaur was trying to steal the eggs for food.

"Did they ever find a dinosaur…" Jet interrupted, then paused while he thought of the word. "I mean… an embryo inside an egg?"

Yes, but not Roy Andrews' group. That is another story. About 70 years later, another group of scientists found an egg in the Gobi Desert that contained bones from an embryo. This embryo resembled an Oviraptor. They realized that the Oviraptor was protecting its own nest of eggs, not trying to steal them, as they had originally assumed.

"Did they find other fossils?" Scout asked waving her hands in excitement.

Yes. Roy Andrews and his group of scientists and paleontologists found many fossils. They found other dinosaur skeletons, big and small. Roy also discovered the first species of Protoceratops, which was later named in his honor: Protoceratops Andrewsi. And they found the first velociraptor specimen.

Scout waited. Somehow, she knew that more was coming. As the words began to appear again, she continued to read aloud.

One of their most amazing discoveries was a small skull, which belonged to one of the earliest known mammals.

"A mammal, as in a cat or dog?" asked Jet in surprise.

Yes, but they didn't find cats and dogs. This specimen was about the size of a rat. Their discovery suggested that small mammals lived in the dinosaur world. This mammal lived around 80 million years ago.

"Wow!" Scout said.

"Why the Gobi Desert?" Scout asked. "I mean, why go there? Roy did say that it was full of treasure."

It's a very important place. Some people thought that the Gobi Desert would contain some of the Earth's earliest life forms. Dinosaurs roamed there approximately 100 million years ago. Scientists still go on expeditions in the Gobi Desert. It is full of treasure.

"What was the Gobi like in the past?" Scout asked. "I mean, before Roy's expedition?"

It was a different climate 120 million years ago. There were rivers and lakes and plants.

"Who was Roy, anyway?" Jet wanted more information.

"And did he really hate snakes?" Scout chimed in.

Roy Chapman Andrews (1884-1960) was a scientist and an explorer. He worked at the

American Museum of Natural History. In the
1920s, he gathered an expedition of scientists
to search the Gobi Desert for fossils. In 1935,
he became the museum's director.

Jet and Scout were taking in all the information,
but the book continued.

Have you heard of Indiana Jones?

Jet and Scout looked at each other. "Yes," said
Scout. "We love those movies."

Many believe that Roy Andrews inspired one
of the most popular film series of all time:
Indiana Jones, by George Lucas and Steven
Spielberg. They are many similarities. Like
Indiana Jones, Roy Andrews wore a ranger
hat. And he almost always carried a revolver.
He had a lot of adventures – and he did not
like snakes.

"So cool," said Jet. Scout nodded with enthusiasm. The book was really on a roll.

Here is a quote from Roy Chapman Andrews: "I was born to be an explorer. There never was any decision to make. I couldn't be anything else and be happy, the desire to see new places, to discover new facts – the curiosity of life always has been a resistless driving force to me."

Scout pondered the quote. Jet thought this was the best day ever. Scout waited a few minutes in case the book continued writing. Nothing happened. The pages were blank.

"Okay," said Scout. "Let's put this book back in the cave while it's still daylight. I want to head back to the cottage." Jet nodded in agreement. His stomach was growling. Scout gently closed the book.

As the cottage came within sight, they walked in silence, reflecting on their adventure.

CHAPTER 5

"**G**ood morning, you two!" their mother said cheerily. "Where are you running off to in such a hurry?" Scout and Jet rushed toward the back door of the cottage.

"We're going on an adventure!" Jet said, before Scout could answer.

"Who knows what we might encounter." Scout said as she finished tying her shoes.

"Yeah," said Jet, as he ran out the door. "Vipers or even bandits."

"That's… um… quite the imagination." Their mother looked up from her coffee, smiling and shaking her head.

Charm held the back door open for Scout. "Ah, yes, vipers." Charm's voice was barely louder that the wind chimes swaying outside the door. "Vipers are huge snakes. Hopefully you will come across something less scary… like dinosaur eggs." Charm winked at Scout.

Scout gasped and looked up at Charm. Scout was about to ask her a question, but then changed her mind. Her eyes scanned the horizon and she saw Jet in the distance.

"Wait for me, Jet! And we are not looking for snakes!" she hollered.

SCOUT&JET

SCOUT&JET
INTO THE GOBI DESERT

OTHER SCOUT & JET BOOKS:
THE ADVENTURE BEGINS

COMING SOON:
INTO EGYPT

A Little PhDs Book
www.littlephds.com

ABOUT THE AUTHOR

Theophany Eystathioy has a PhD and has worked extensively in the field of cellular and molecular biology. Formerly an adjunct professor at the University of Calgary and a technology analyst in intellectual property, Theophany lives with her husband and her two children. Her goal is to share the fun and curiosity of science with kids of all ages, while fostering a lifelong love of this fascinating subject.

CPSIA information can be obtained
at www.ICGtesting.com
Printed in the USA
LVOW13s0201051116
511740LV00002B/2/P